IRAQ
the culture

April Fast

A Bobbie Kalman Book
The Lands, Peoples, and Cultures Series

Crabtree Publishing Company

www.crabtreebooks.com

The Lands, Peoples, and Cultures Series

Created by Bobbie Kalman

Author: April Fast

Third edition: Q2AMedia

Editor: Adrianna Morganelli

Content and Photo editor: Kokila Manchanda

Editorial director: Kathy Middleton

Production coordinator: Margaret Salter

Prepress technician: Margaret Salter

Project manager: Kumar Kanul

First and second editions
   Coordinating editor: Ellen Rodger
   Project editor: Rachel Eagen
   Production coordinator: Rosie Gowsell
   Project development: First Folio Resource Group, Inc.
   Photo research: Maria DeCambra
   Consultants: Thabit Abdullah, Department of History,
      York University; Majid Aziza

Cover: A man carries an illuminated model of a mosque on his head, which weighs about 550 pounds (250 kg), as an act of thanks and devotion, during the religious festival of Ashura outside the Imam al-Kadhum shrine in Baghdad.

Title page: Kurdish girls dressed in traditional clothing dance with other villagers of Karkush, east of Mosul.

Back cover: Carp swim in almost every stream, river, and lake in Iraq, and they are raised on fish farms. Most carp caught in Iraq are eaten locally.

Icon: Ziggurats, which had temples at the very top, were built in ancient Mesopotamia to honor gods and connect heaven and earth.

Illustrations:
Dianne Eastman: icon
David Wysotski, Allure Illustrations: back cover
Blair Drawson: p. 30–31

Photographs:
AFP: Ali Al-Saadi: p. 13 (top); Nicolas Asfouri: p. 17 (right)
AP Photo: Brennan Linsley: p. 12 (bottom); Hussein Malla: p. 8; Jassim
   Mohammed: p. 10; Muhammed Muheisen: p. 26 (top); Pressens
   Bild/Jonas Ekstomer: p. 29 (left); Ivan Sekretarev: title page,
   p. 17 (left); Murad Sezer: p. 25 (bottom); Alexander Zemlianichenko:
   p. 9 (bottom); Vahid Salemi: p. 7 (bottom); Loay Hameed: p. 15
   (bottom); Mohammed Hato: p. 23 (bottom)
Art Directors: Jane Sweeney: p. 20 (top right)
Art Resource, NY: p. 19 (right), p. 21 (right); Erich Lessing: p. 19 (left);
   Réunion des Musées Nationaux: p. 24 (both), p. 25 (bottom); Scala:
   p. 4 (top), p. 6 (left), p. 21 (left), p. 22 (right), p. 25 (top)
Atlas Geographic: Fatih Pinar: p. 9 (top)
Bridgeman Art Library: Roger Perrin: p. 28;
Corbis: Lynsey Addario/Magma: p. 11 (bottom), p. 15 (top); Thorne
   Anderson/Magma: p. 7 (top); Françoise de Mulder/Magma:
   p. 5 (top); Antoine Gyori/France Reportage/Magma: p. 12 (top);
   Charles & Josette Lenars/Magma: p. 3; Patrick Robert/Magma:
   p. 23 (top); David Turnley/Magma: p. 20 (bottom left); Nik
   Wheeler/Magma: p. 6 (right); Michael S. Yamashita/Magma:
   p. 22 (left)
Getty Images: Ahmad Al-Rubaye/AFP: p. 16 (left); Timothy A.
   Clary/AFP: p. 18 (right); Maxim Marmur/AFP: p. 27
Ivy Images: Nik Wheeler: p. 13 (right);
Photolibrary: Caroline Penn: p. 4 (bottom),
Reuters: Khaled al-Hariri: p. 5 (bottom); Mohamed Hammi: p. 18 (left);
   Ali Jarekji: p. 16 (right); Thaier Al-Sudani: p. 11 (top); Nikola Solic:
   p. 14; Ali Jasim: cover

Library and Archives Canada Cataloguing in Publication

Fast, April, 1968-
   Iraq : the culture / April Fast. -- Rev. ed.

(Lands, peoples, and cultures series)
Includes index.
ISBN 978-0-7787-9281-9 (bound)--ISBN 978-0-7787-9651-0 (pbk.).

   1. Iraq--Social life and customs--Juvenile literature.
2. Iraq--Civilization--Juvenile literature. I. Title.
II. Series: Lands, peoples, and cultures series

DS70.7.F28 2010   j956.7   C2009-905133-8

Library of Congress Cataloging-in-Publication Data

Fast, April, 1968-
   Iraq, the culture / April Fast. -- Rev. ed.
      p. cm. -- (The lands, peoples, and cultures series)
   "A Bobbie Kalman Book."
   Includes index.
   ISBN 978-0-7787-9651-0 (pbk. : alk. paper) -- ISBN 978-0-7787-9281-9 (reinforced
library binding : alk. paper)
   1. Iraq--Civilization--Juvenile literature. I. Title. II. Series.

DS70.7.F35 2010
956.7--dc22

                                                  2009034655

Crabtree Publishing Company
www.crabtreebooks.com   1-800-387-7650

Printed in China/122009/CT20090915

Published in Canada
Crabtree Publishing
616 Welland Ave.
St. Catharines, ON
L2M 5V6

Published in the United States
Crabtree Publishing
PMB 59051
350 Fifth Avenue, 59th Floor
New York, New York 10118

Published in the United Kingdom
Crabtree Publishing
Maritime House
Basin Road North, Hove
BN41 1WR

Published in Australia
Crabtree Publishing
386 Mt. Alexander Rd.
Ascot Vale (Melbourne)
VIC 3032

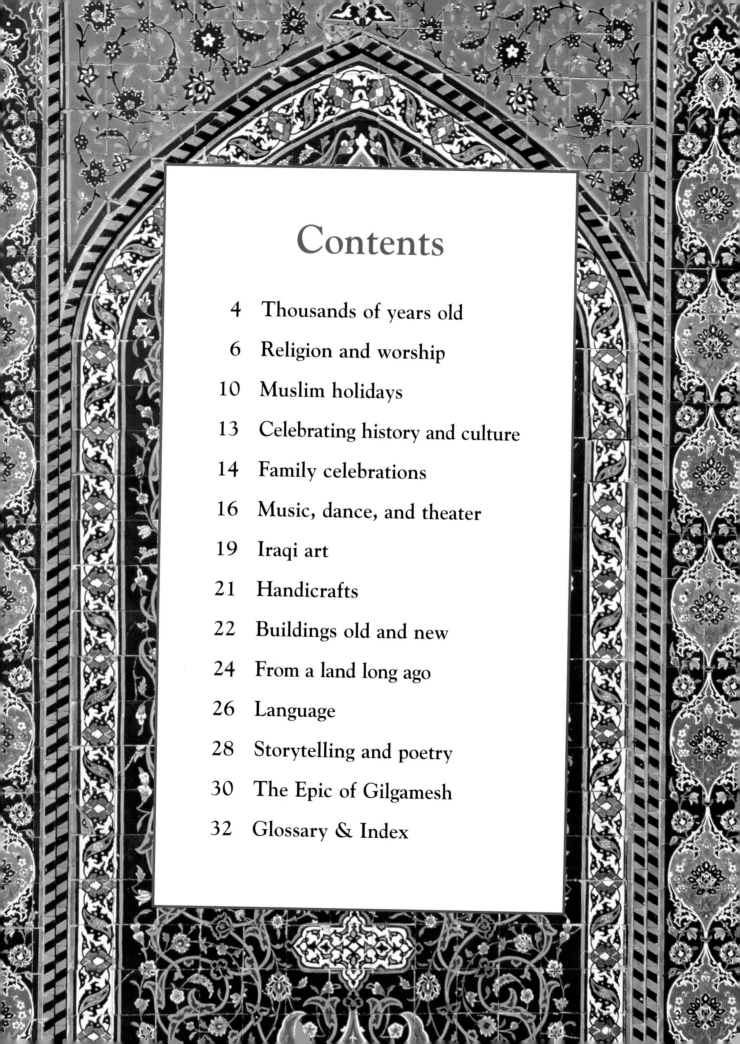

Contents

Thousands of years old

The country of Iraq lies in the Middle East, which is the area surrounding the southern and eastern shores of the Mediterranean Sea. Modern Iraq is less than 100 years old, yet people have lived on its land for more than twelve thousand years.

Iraq is in a region that was once known as Mesopotamia, from the Greek words for "land between the rivers." The rivers are the Tigris and Euphrates, which sustained life for peoples such as the Sumerians, Akkadians, and Babylonians long ago. Today, Iraq is home to Arabs, Kurds, Assyrians, Armenians, Turkmen, and other **ethnic** groups, who thrive on this ancient land and contribute to the country's rich culture.

(above) Colorful tiles decorate a shrine, or holy site, of a Muslim religious leader. Shrines attract millions of faithful visitors each year.

(top) The ancient Babylonian king Nebuchadnezzar II built a 700-room palace that was guarded by the Ishtar Gate. The gate was decorated with brick images of bulls, dragons, and other mythical creatures.

Shaped like an egg split open, the Martyrs' Monument in Baghdad was constructed in memory of the hundreds of thousands of Iraqi soldiers who died in the Iran-Iraq War. The war was fought between 1980 and 1988. Inside the monument are the names, weapons, and clothing of some of the soldiers.

The influence of Saddam Hussein

From 1979 to 2003, Iraq was led by Saddam Hussein. Hussein was head of a political party called the Arab Ba'th Socialist Party. In many ways, Hussein seemed to be a great supporter of his country's culture. He opened museums, funded a national symphony, and introduced festivals that celebrated the country's rich past. However, Hussein also wanted to keep firm control over the people of Iraq. He **censored** or banned books, movies, newspapers, and art that he felt criticized him and his government. He also outlawed some religious and political holidays for fear that a gathering of people would turn into a public protest against him.

Hussein's government fell apart during a war fought against an American-led **coalition** in 2003. Iraq's future is uncertain, but the people are beginning to recover their freedoms and many aspects of their culture. They are celebrating holidays that were once banned, enjoying music and films that were forbidden, and expressing their hopes for better times ahead through works of art and literature.

Many artists, writers, and musicians left Iraq during Saddam Hussein's rule because they were not allowed to express themselves freely. Famous Iraqi musician Sahar Taha, who moved to Lebanon, a country that borders the Mediterranean Sea, sings old folk songs accompanied by an instrument called an oud.

The Sumerians, who settled in southern Mesopotamia around 3500 B.C., believed that Abu, the god of vegetation who is depicted in this sculpture, controlled all plant life.

The ancient Mesopotamians believed gods and goddesses controlled the world around them. These gods included Enlil, the storm god; Shamash, also called Utu, the sun god; Sin, also called Nanna, the moon god; and Ishtar, the goddess of **fertility**. The people of each town and city worshiped one main god and built a **temple** in the god's honor. They prayed in the temple and made **sacrifices** before a statue that they believed held the spirit of the god.

Islam

Today, more than 97 percent of Iraqis are Muslims, or followers of the religion of Islam. The **prophet** Muhammad spread this religion around 610 A.D., after receiving the teachings of Allah, the Arabic word for God. Allah's teachings were whispered to him by the angel Jibril and recorded in the Muslim holy book, the *Qur'an*.

Iraqi Muslims pray in mosques, such as this one in the southern city of Basra. If a mosque is not close by, they pray at home, at work, at school, or wherever they happen to be.

About 50,000 Muslim worshipers bend in prayer outside the Hekma mosque in an area called Al Thawra, or Sadr City, in the capital, Baghdad.

The Five Pillars of Islam

There are five main teachings of Islam, known as the Five Pillars of Islam:

- Muslims must declare that there is only one God and that Muhammad is his prophet.
- Muslims must pray five times a day: before sunrise, in the early afternoon, in the late afternoon, after sunset, and at night.
- Muslims who can afford to do so must give to those in need.
- Healthy Muslims must not eat or drink from dawn until dusk during the Muslim month of *Ramadan*.
- At least once in their lifetime, healthy and able Muslims must make a **pilgrimage**, known as *hajj*, to the holy city of Mecca in Saudi Arabia.

Shia and Sunnis

All Muslims follow the Five Pillars of Islam, but there are two main Muslim groups in Iraq with slightly different beliefs: Shia and Sunnis. Almost 65 percent of Iraqi Muslims are Shia. They live in the central and southern regions of Iraq. The rest are Sunnis, who live mostly in central and northern Iraq.

The division between Shia and Sunnis developed after the prophet Muhammad died. The Shia wanted the future caliphs, or spiritual and political leaders of Islam, to be descendants of Muhammad's cousin and son-in-law, Ali. The Sunnis believed that the caliphs should be elected from among Muhammad's closest followers. This division led to the groups developing their own *Sunna*, or codes of behavior.

Sufism

Some Iraqi Muslims also practice the tradition of Sufism, a blend of Muslim and ancient **mystical** ideas. Sufis seek to become closer to God through **reflection**, music, and poetry. They belong to groups called brotherhoods, each of which has its own **rituals** and customs.

Pilgrimages

Iraqis, mainly Shia Muslims, make pilgrimages to holy cities in their country to show their devotion to religious leaders who are buried there. Entire families travel by car, bus, or plane to cities such as Najaf, Karbala, and Samarra to pray at mosques and **shrines**.

Iraqis also go on pilgrimage, or *hajj*, to Mecca, the holy city in Saudi Arabia. Most pilgrims to Mecca are adults, although children as young as 12 make the journey. Those who complete the *hajj* are honored with the title of *hajia,* for a woman, or *haji,* for a man.

Shia pilgrims pray at the shrine of Imam Hussein in Karbala.

Christianity

Some peoples in Iraq follow the religion of Christianity. They observe the teachings of Jesus Christ, who they believe is God's son. Most Assyrians in Iraq follow a branch of Christianity called the Christian Nestorian Church. Other Assyrians belong to the Roman Catholic Church. Armenians, who live mainly in the capital city of Baghdad, follow either the Armenian branch of the Roman Catholic Church or the Armenian Apostolic Church.

(top) Assyrian women light candles at a Catholic church after an Easter Mass, or religious service.

Christian holidays

Christians in Iraq celebrate many of the same holidays as Christians in other parts of the world. Christmas celebrates Jesus' birth, and Easter marks his death and resurrection, or rebirth. Iraqi Christians also celebrate Holy Cross Day on September 14. The holiday honors a Christian empress who lived long ago. She asked her people to find the cross on which Jesus was crucified, or put to death. Once the people were satisfied that the true cross had been found, they burned all the false ones. On Holy Cross Day, Christians in Iraq light bonfires of thorn bushes and jump over the ashes three times making a wish.

A Yezidi religious leader lights holy candles in preparation for a ceremony that honors Malak Taus.

Yezidi beliefs

Yezidis, most of whom belong to an ethnic group known as the Kurds, live in the hills of northwestern Iraq. Yezidis combine Christian, **pagan**, **Zoroastrian**, and Muslim beliefs. They honor both the *Qur'an* and the Christian Bible, but they also follow their own religious texts. They believe that seven angels, led by Malak Taus, the peacock angel, control life on Earth.

Mandaeans

Around 4,000 to 5,000 Mandaeans live in Iraq, mainly in Baghdad and the south. Their religion, called Mandaeanism, is older than Christianity. It combines ancient Mesopotamian beliefs with the teachings of the prophet John the Baptist. Mandaeans are also called Sabians, which means "those who **baptize**" in the Aramaic language, because they believe that water has the power to give life. Their prayers, teachings, and beliefs are found in a holy book called the *Ginza Raba*, meaning "great treasure."

Mandaeans practice ritual baptism on the banks of the Tigris River.

Muslim holidays

For most aspects of life, Iraqis follow the Gregorian calendar, which is the same calendar North Americans use. The Gregorian, or solar, calendar follows the cycles of the earth around the sun. For religious holidays, Iraqis follow the Muslim calendar, which is a lunar calendar. In the lunar calendar, a new month begins when a full moon appears.

Ramadan

During the ninth month of the Muslim calendar, Muslims honor the time when the angel Jibril whispered the words of Allah into Muhammad's ear. During this month, called *Ramadan*, Muslims do not eat or drink between dawn and dusk. They fast to build self-discipline, and to be free to focus on Allah and his many blessings. Fasting is also thought to teach compassion for those who go hungry. Only pregnant women, young children, the elderly, and the ill do not fast. Most children begin fasting during *Ramadan* when they are 13 years old.

In many Iraqi cities, a loud drumbeat before dawn marks the start of each day of *Ramadan*. Most Muslims wake up at this time to eat a meal called *suhur* before the fast begins. The firing of a cannon marks the end of the fast each day. Muslims then eat a meal called *iftar*, which traditionally begins with a date, followed by milk, water, and a bowl of soup. It is said that the prophet Muhammad fasted after receiving the first message from Allah, then broke his fast by eating a date.

Eid al-Fitr

Eid al-Fitr is a three-day celebration marking the end of *Ramadan*. *Eid al-Fitr* means "the festival of fast breaking." All businesses close, and homes and streets are decorated with lights or tiny, colorful flags. People spend *Eid al-Fitr* praying, visiting family and friends, and sharing large meals. Children receive gifts of money or new clothing, and girls decorate their hands and feet with the bright dye of the henna plant.

(top) After the sun sets, the Ramadan *fast is broken with a meal called* iftar.

Eid al-Adha

At the end of *hajj*, the yearly pilgrimage to Mecca, Muslims celebrate *Eid al-Adha*. This four-day festival honors the prophet Ibrahim, who was willing to prove his faith to Allah by sacrificing his only son, Ishmael. Just before Ibrahim carried out Allah's wishes, Allah showed mercy on him and allowed him to sacrifice a lamb instead.

On *Eid al-Adha*, Iraqi Muslims wear their best clothing and go to the mosque in the morning for *Salat al-Eid*, or Eid Prayer. Then, they gather at home for festive meals. Many families roast a lamb to remember the lamb that Ibrahim sacrificed, and distribute one third of the meat to those in need. The rest is shared among family and friends.

(above) During Eid al-Fitr, *neighborhoods come alive with fairs, street parties, and sometimes weddings.*

A boy selects a sheep to be slaughtered for the Eid al-Adha *holiday dinner.*

11

Thousands of Shia visit Karbala to pray and mourn at the site where Imam Hussein is buried.

Ashura

Ashura is a time of mourning observed by Shia in honor of the religious leader Imam Hussein, the grandson of the prophet Muhammad. **Rival** Muslims killed Hussein in a battle near the Iraqi city of Karbala in 680 A.D., on the tenth day of *Muharram*. *Muharram* is the first month of the Muslim calendar.

On each of the first ten nights of *Muharram*, Shia gather to hear the story of the last ten days of Imam Hussein and his companions. The story ends on the tenth day, *Ashura*, with the tale of Hussein's bravery and death in battle. Men parade through the streets, striking their chests or beating themselves with chains, belts, and sticks to recall Hussein's suffering. The story of Hussein is reenacted in dramatic, emotional plays. The actor playing Hussein wears green, the international color of Islam. His enemies wear red.

On Ashura, Shia say special prayers in memory of Imam Hussein. At all times, men and women pray in separate sections at mosques.

Mawlid al-Nabi

Mawlid al-Nabi celebrates the birth of Muhammad, on the twelfth day of the third month, which is called *Rabi' al-Awal*. On this day, Sunnis gather at mosques or in homes to tell stories about Muhammad's birth, read about his life and teachings, and reflect on how well they have followed these teachings in their own lives.

Members of one of Iraq's political parties, the Iraqi Communist Party, celebrate the anniversary of the 1958 Revolution after the fall of Saddam Hussein. They had not been allowed to celebrate this holiday since the Ba'th Party came to power in 1968.

The anniversaries of important dates in Iraq's history are times of celebration. On July 14, Iraqis celebrated the 1958 Revolution Anniversary. This marked the day that a group of young military officers, known as the Free Officers, overthrew the **monarchy** that had ruled Iraq since just after it became a country in 1920. The officers declared Iraq a **republic**, and a new period of freedom began for Iraqis.

When the Ba'th Party seized power in 1968, it abolished the 1958 Revolution Anniversary and established a new Revolution Anniversary, on July 17, to honor the beginning of its rule. After the fall of Saddam Hussein's government, the coalition government abolished this holiday as well as five others that the Ba'th Party created. Still, many Iraqis celebrate July 17 as an important day in their history.

New Year's celebrations

Iraqis celebrate two New Year's days. The first day of *Muharram*, which is the first month of the Muslim calendar, is a day off from work and the beginning of the period leading to *Ashura*.

Some Iraqis also celebrate New Year's Eve on December 31, the end of the year according to the Gregorian calendar. They hold parties and feasts, and count down to the new year.

Nawruz

Traditionally, Kurds follow a version of the solar calendar called *shamsi*. According to *shamsi*, the new year begins at the time of the spring **equinox**, which usually falls on March 21.

The festival of *Nawruz* marks the Kurdish new year and welcomes spring. Kurds light bonfires a few days before *Nawruz* to signify the end of winter and the beginning of the season of light. During the week-long festivities, they resolve misunderstandings with one another and give each other presents. They also enjoy picnics, parades, dances, plays, poetry recitals, and fireworks.

Girls wearing colorful costumes march in a Nawruz, or Kurdish new year parade.

For many Iraqis, family pride and honor are more important than personal success. Each member of a Muslim family is expected to follow a code of behavior, which includes **modesty** for women and observance of Muslim laws. People must strive to avoid bringing shame or embarrassment on their family through poor behavior.

Al-khatma

Muslims believe that being able to read the *Qur'an* is important if a person is to receive Allah's blessings. The *al-khatma* is a ceremony held by traditional, religious families in Iraq to celebrate the first time a child reads from the *Qur'an* without making mistakes. There is no set age for attempting the *al-khatma*. Whenever a child is ready, he or she begins taking classes with a religious tutor, and studies for more than a year. The *al-khatma* takes place in the presence of family and friends and is followed by a tea or lunch. A child who has read the *al-khatma* is honored with the title of *hafiz* or *hafiza*, which means "one who remembers."

Marriage

Traditionally, marriages in Iraq are arranged, which means that two families decide together that their children should marry. Iraqis see marriage as a way of joining two families, not just two people, and family background and honor are important in deciding on a match. According to custom, the groom's family gives the new bride a **dowry**, called the *muqaddam*, which consists of money, jewels, household items, or even water buffalo. A second dowry, called the *mu'akhar*, is money that the groom's family puts aside for the bride in case she and her husband divorce.

Iraqi wedding celebrations usually last two or three days. The bride is brought from her home to the groom's home, where the ceremony takes place. After the ceremony, a jug is broken to "break evil," since clay pots are traditionally believed to contain evil spirits. The party that follows, with large meals, music, and dancing, is also held at the groom's home, but some very wealthy families host the party in a rented hall.

(top) Iraqis traditionally believe that demons can steal a beautiful child, so they are careful not to fuss too much over a baby's beauty. Most Iraqi families hang an eye symbol over a baby's bed to keep jealousy and evil spirits away.

Today, more and more Iraqis choose their own spouses, especially among less traditional families in cities, although parents often "arrange" the wedding by discussing it together before the engagement is official.

Mandaean weddings

Mandaeans, whose belief system revolves around water and baptism, hold ritual baptisms for the bride and groom at a riverbank. After being baptized, the bride and groom wear white as a symbol of purity and stand under a hut made of reeds and palm fronds. During the wedding ceremony, the couple eats food from a set of special clay bowls and drinks grape or date juice. The religious leader gently knocks their heads together three times to help ensure a close and faithful marriage, and declares them married.

Mourning loved ones

According to Muslim tradition, a person who has died is washed and draped in a *kafan*, or plain white sheet, and buried within 24 hours, with his or her head facing the holy city of Mecca. After the funeral is a period of mourning which lasts 40 days. Friends and relatives visit the grieving family at the start and end of the mourning period to pray and offer comfort.

Members of a funeral procession carry a casket to a burial site in Sadr City, Baghdad.

Music, dance, and theater

Musicians in the southern port of Basra perform a traditional sea shanty, a type of song that sailors used to sing while working on ships.

In ancient Mesopotamia, musicians played for the gods in temples, entertained in kings' courts, and performed in public squares. Popular instruments included **lyres**, harps, tambourines, drums, cymbals, and flutes. Today, musicians performing traditional Iraqi songs play the *oud*, a stringed instrument with a short neck and three sound holes; the *kanoun*, a type of harp that sounds like a xylophone and an electric guitar combined; and the *rebab*, a two-stringed instrument with a thick body.

Traditional Arab music

Bedouin music is the oldest type of folk music in the Arab world. The Bedouin, who are traditionally a **nomadic** people, tell stories of love, freedom, and suffering in their songs. The women are the main singers. They perform special songs to mark weddings, births, and anniversaries, and to ward off evil spirits at mosques and shrines. Most of the songs are soft and gentle, although singers ululate, or create piercing howl sounds in the back of their throats, to show great joy or sorrow. Traditional Bedouin music is beginning to find its way back into the popular culture of Iraq.

Classical Iraqi music

The traditional music of Iraq is the *maqam*. *Maqam* songs are based on Arabic poetry and are very heart-wrenching and slow. *Maqam* musical scales are believed to have developed in the courts of ancient Arabian kings, and been influenced by Persian, or the culture of Iran.

Maqam singers often add **improvisation** to their well-known melodies and create songs that feel like a conversation. There is constant interaction between the singer and the audience, who yell "Repeat!" or "Chorus!" to direct the singer. At the end of a *maqam* performance, the lead singer rests and the audience sings the final song. A young **apprentice** of the singer sometimes watches the entire performance from the audience, imitating the singer and preparing for his or her time in the spotlight.

Farida Mohammed Ali and her Iraqi Maqam Ensemble perform traditional maqam *songs.*

(left) Festive gouranis have strong, exciting rhythms and are often accompanied by dancing and clapping. They are played at weddings and other celebrations.

(below) Performers dance at the National Theater in Baghdad to celebrate the founding of Baghdad in the 700s.

Kurdish music

Kurdish music of long ago described the sadness of life, but over time the music took on a more upbeat, joyous quality. There are two forms of Kurdish music. The first is improvised music and is known as *maqam*, but it is much faster than the classical Iraqi *maqam*. The second form of Kurdish music is called *gourani*. There are *gouranis* for different occasions. Children's *gouranis* are based on children's poems and have very simple rhythms. Women sing women's *gouranis* alone or in groups during their everyday chores. *Ramadan gouranis* announce the start of the daily fast during the month of *Ramadan*.

Traditional dance

Dance has played an important role in Iraqi culture for thousands of years. The *hacha'a* is a popular dance among Arabs. It is similar to belly dancing, but there is more neck and hand motion and less hip movement. A woman dances the *hacha'a* alone, as a drummer moves around her. A *hacha'a* dancer must have long hair, because part of the dance involves swinging her hair to the music.

Dance is also important to Kurdish culture. One popular Kurdish dance is the *dabka*, in which dancers in a line move their shoulders and stomp the ground rhythmically.

Modern music

Beginning in the late 1940s, Iraqi musicians began adding livelier rhythms and lighter melodies to *maqam* songs, creating a type of traditional sounding pop music. Gradually, different styles of music from other Arab countries blended into Iraqi music. Then, in the late 1970s, European and North American styles of music started to influence the musical tastes of Iraqis. Today, people in Iraq enjoy both traditional songs and western pop music.

During the rule of Saddam Hussein, musicians were expected to praise him in their songs. Today, many Iraqi performers sing about the effects of war in their country and the difficulties that people face every day. Some musicians have left Iraq, but continue to make music that reflects their origins. Kazem al-Saher, who is now a Canadian citizen, sings pop songs based on classical Iraqi music that tell of life before war and life in Iraq today. Ilham al-Madfa'i, who lives in the United States, sings modern versions of old folk songs accompanied by Spanish guitar, electric guitar, and saxophone.

An Armenian violinist rehearses for a performance with the Iraqi National Symphony Orchestra in Baghdad.

Iraqi theater

Theater was a popular form of entertainment before the Ba'th Party came to power, but it was heavily censored under Saddam Hussein. During his rule, plays could only be performed if they praised Hussein. Today, groups such as Baghdad's National Theater company are hoping to bring plays about a range of topics back to the Iraqi people. Children's puppet plays are being enjoyed at festivals and special celebrations throughout the countryside. One popular puppet play is *Layla and the Wolf*, a version of *Little Red Riding Hood*.

Kazem al-Saher is one of Iraq's most popular singers. He is famous for his beautiful love ballads, but he is also a well-respected poet and composer.

Miniature paintings

Beginning in the late 1100s, painters in Baghdad became known for their small, colorful drawings, called miniature paintings. Miniature paintings decorated medical texts, books about animals, volumes of poetry, and adventure stories. One of the most famous painters of miniatures was Yahya al-Wasiti, who lived in the 1200s. His drawings depicted **architecture**, furnishings, weapons, and costumes from that time.

The earliest Mesopotamian art, from around 6000 B.C., included statues of gods made of gold, silver, and bronze. Thousands of years later, the Assyrians, whose empire reached the height of its power between 900 B.C. and 600 B.C., created stone carvings, called bas-reliefs, that depicted hunts, feasts, and military victories. They also created murals of brightly colored glazed bricks, and they carved ivory into jewelry and decorations for royal thrones.

(top) This stone relief, which once decorated the palace of Ashurbanipal in the Assyrian capital of Nineveh, shows archers fighting. The Assyrians were known as powerful warriors.

(above) This painting by Yahya al-Wasiti decorated the Maqamat, a collection of witty stories written in rhyme by the author al-Hariri.

Later Muslim art

Religious leaders instructed later Muslim artists not to depict people in their work because they believed that only Allah created life. Instead, many artists decorated buildings with floral and geometric designs made from small ceramic tiles. The buildings were also decorated with the words of the *Qur'an* in an artistic handwriting called calligraphy.

Expressionism

Iraq's modern art movement began in the early 1900s when the **Ottomans** controlled the land that became Iraq. Military officers who trained at Ottoman schools in Istanbul, Turkey's capital, were taught how to use oil paints. Once King Faisal came to power in the 1920s, he arranged for Iraqi artists to study in Europe during the time of an artistic movement called expressionism. Artists painting in an expressionist style experimented with color and form, and depicted feelings rather than realistic scenes.

The Monument for Freedom, in Baghdad, was created by Jawad Salim. It tells of the 1958 Revolution, when Iraq's monarchy was overthrown.

Modern art

In 1950, a group of self-taught Iraqi artists and art-school graduates formed La Société Primitive, later named the Pioneers. These artists moved their studios outside to paint what they saw in nature and in city streets. The Baghdad Group of Modern Art was established by the painter and sculptor Jawad Salim in 1951. Salim's group combined techniques borrowed from ancient art with those of cubism, a style of art in which objects look as if they are broken into small pieces and stuck back together again.

Portrait of a ruler

During Saddam Hussein's rule, government officials paid artists to create works that **glorified** Iraq and its leaders. Many of these works were portraits of Saddam Hussein. Enormous posters, murals, and sculptures of Hussein were found on buildings, in parks, and in city squares. Since Hussein's government was overthrown, many of these pieces of art have been taken down by Iraqis and by coalition troops in the country.

Many murals depicted Saddam Hussein as an approachable leader who cared for all members of society.

In Mesopotamia, potters created pitchers, bowls, and other useful objects.

Craftspeople who lived in Iraq thousands of years ago made bowls, plates, and vases from bronze or clay. Today, pots and other household items are made of copper or clay. The clay is usually painted in rich, bold colors and decorated with pictures of fish and horseshoes, which are both believed to bring good luck.

Working in metal and wood

Iraqi **artisans** craft beautiful jewelry from silver, gold, and copper. The Mandaeans also use lapis lazuli, a deep blue gemstone from the Middle East, in their work. Many artisans carve wood into vases, chandeliers, pipes, and small boxes. The Ma'dan, an Arabic people who live in Iraq's southern marshes, are famous for their wooden canoes.

Weavings

Iraqi artisans weave blankets, curtains, and clothing out of wool, felt, silk, and mohair, which is the hair of the Angora goat. Mats, baskets, purses, and even chairs are woven from palm branches and wheat stalks. Woolen carpets are among Iraq's most famous weavings. In Mesopotamia, wealthy families often hired craftspeople to weave carpets with unique designs. Today, carpets are sold to other countries as well as in local stores and markets called *souks*.

Iraqi carpets are decorated with geometric patterns, which vary from region to region, in bright reds, oranges, browns, yellows, and blues.

The Sumerian king Ur-Nammu built this ziggurat in Ur in honor of Sin, the moon god, around 2100 B.C. The ziggurat stands about 70 feet (21 meters) above the desert.

Iraq is rich in architecture dating back thousands of years. Over time, ancient temples and palaces, as well as the homes of farmers, craftspeople, and merchants, were abandoned. Many were buried beneath sand and mud from storms and floods. **Archaeologists** are slowly uncovering these buildings, and Iraqi architects are borrowing from their designs as they plan new structures.

Ziggurats
The word "ziggurat" comes from a Babylonian word that means "to build high." Ziggurats were temples made of two to seven tiers, or layers, each level smaller than the one below. The outside of each tier was glazed a different color: red to represent the **underworld**, black to represent the earth, blue to represent the sky, and gold to represent the sun. The highest tier was topped with a shrine dedicated to the local god.

The Kadhimiya Mosque, in Baghdad, was built in 1515 to honor two Shi'i imams. It is decorated with intricate tilework, and its two domes and the tops of its four minarets are guilded, or coated with gold.

Shrines and mosques
Iraq's many shrines and mosques house the tombs of religious leaders and serve as centers of worship. One of Iraq's most famous mosques is the Great Mosque of Samarra, an ancient city north of Baghdad. The mosque was built in the late 800s and has a spiral minaret, or tower, that rises 170 feet (52 meters) high. The nearby Askari Shrine is the burial site of an important religious leader, called an *imam*. Its gilded dome is one of the largest in the Muslim world.

Palaces

The kings and leaders of Mesopotamia and modern Iraq have always built magnificent palaces to live in. Isa ibn Musa, a wealthy prince, built Ukhaydir Palace in the desert southwest of Karbala in the late 700s. The **fortified** complex included a mosque, palace, and bathhouse, or separate building for bathing.

In 1982, Saddam Hussein rebuilt the Babylon palace of King Nebuchadnezzar II, who ruled from 605 to 562 B.C. Archaeologists disagreed with the project because they believed it would ruin the ancient site. Hussein also built a new palace for himself in Babylon, with high ceilings, spiral staircases, arched entryways, endless marble, and exquisite furniture. Since the overthrow of his government, thieves have stripped the palace of many of its treasures.

Modern architecture

The best examples of modern architecture in Iraq are in Baghdad. The designs of many of the city's art galleries, museums, hotels, and public libraries are inspired by Muslim architecture. Muslim architecture is famous for its use of domes and gilding, along with colorful tile **mosaics**, pillars, arches, and stonework.

(above) Saddam Hussein built 55 lavish palaces during his rule, which lasted from 1979 to 2003. The presidential complex in Tikrit, in northern Iraq, is composed of several palaces built next to the Tigris River. The site was destroyed in April 2003 by U.S. warplanes.

(below) In the 1700s and 1800s, some homes in Baghdad, Mosul, and Basra had screened balconies called shanashils. The screens were often made of wood carved into delicate patterns. Many of these homes still stand today.

The ancient Mesopotamians were great creators and inventors. The Sumerians, who ruled from about 3500 B.C. to 2300 B.C., are believed to have invented the wheel and the 12-month calendar. Each month began when the first sliver of a new moon appeared.

Cuneiform

Writing was one of Mesopotamia's greatest accomplishments. It was developed by the Sumerians around 3200 B.C. The first writing consisted of pictures that **scribes** etched into wet clay with a pointed instrument called a stylus. The stylus was made from the stems of reeds or pieces of bone or wood. Soon, a wedge-shaped tip replaced the point, and straight lines were drawn instead of complete pictures to save time. This system of lines came to be known as cuneiform, for the **Latin** words *cuneus*, meaning "wedge," and *forma*, meaning "shape."

(top) The earliest cuneiform writings were simple lists or records of traded items, such as animals, grains, or vegetables. Numbers were expressed by repeating lines or circles. This carved tablet is a record of horses and sheep to be sacrificed.

Laws

The Sumerian king Ur-Nammu established some of the first laws in the world around 2050 B.C. Known as the Code of Ur-Nammu, they dealt with topics such as marriage, divorce, theft, injury to others, and owning land. The Babylonian king Hammurabi, who ruled from 1792 to 1750 B.C., wrote his own set of 282 laws, known as the Code of Hammurabi. They were carved on tablets and displayed throughout his empire.

The following are some examples of his laws:
- Law 25: If a fire breaks out in a house and the person who comes to put it out steals the owner's property, the thief shall be thrown into the fire.
- Law 55: If a person opens his ditches to water his crops and the water floods his neighbor's field, he shall pay his neighbor corn for the loss.

(below) This stele, or stone pillar, contains a section of the Code of Hammurabi. At the top of the stele is the sun god Shamash dictating his laws to Hammurabi.

Babylonians used different stones for weighing different items. Many of the stones were finely shaped and polished, such as this weight in the shape of a goose.

Weights and measures

Ancient Mesopotamians developed standard, or widely accepted, ways to weigh and measure goods. This helped keep business fair and easy to understand for traders from different lands. At first, standard weights were based on real items. For example, a "donkey load" was based on how much weight a donkey could carry. Then, the Babylonians developed a system of weighing items against standard-sized stones.

The first known standard tool for measurement was a copper bar called the Cubit of Nippur, developed in 1950 B.C. The bar was about 20 inches (51 centimeters) long and divided into equal portions, like a ruler. The Sumerians also established the length of a foot in 2575 B.C., likely to measure cloth. It remains the oldest standard of length in the world today.

Cylinder seals

Cylinder seals were like miniature rolling pins that were usually made of stone. They were carved with images of gods, religious ceremonies, animals, and plants, as well as hunting scenes. Mesopotamians used the seals from about 3000 B.C. to the end of the 400s A.D. to sign documents written on clay tablets and to mark property. Seals were sometimes rolled onto mud bricks before they hardened to indicate when buildings were constructed and who constructed them. People also wore seals as jewelry, since they were believed to protect against illness and danger.

Sometimes, the figures on cylinder seals were arranged in decorative patterns, but more often they showed an action.

The majority of Iraqis speak Arabic, the language of the *Qur'an*, but many other languages are heard in the country's markets and streets. English is the most common western language in Iraq and is often used along with Arabic as a language of instruction in universities.

Arabic

Arabs conquered Mesopotamia in the 600s A.D., but their language arrived two centuries earlier, as Arabic-speaking tribes began moving into the area. Today, Arabic is the official language of most parts of Iraq. It has 29 letters, 26 consonants, and 3 vowels, and is written from right to left. The languages of neighboring countries have influenced the form of Arabic spoken in Iraq, such as as Persian and Turkish words that became part of the Iraqi vocabulary.

Kurdish

Iraq's Kurds live mainly in a northern part of the country known as the Kurdish Autonomous Region, or Iraqi Kurdistan. The region was set aside in 1974 for Kurds to rule independently.

The official language of the area, Kurdish, is related to ancient Persian languages. There are two main **dialects**, Kurdi, or Sorani, and Kermanji. Kurdi is spoken in the south of Iraqi Kurdistan and is the official form of Kurdish in the region. Kermanji is spoken by Kurds in the north of the region. Both dialects are written in Arabic script in Iraq, and most Kurds can understand both.

(above) Kurdish street vendors have a lively discussion in the shopping district of Irbil, a city in the north.

(top) Students test each other before an exam at the University of Baghdad. In times of peace, many languages can be heard at the university, where students from Iraq as well as other Arab and foreign countries, study.

English	Arabic	Kurdi
Hello.	Marhaba.	Bakher been.
Goodbye.	Maa' elSalama.	Khwa hafiz.
How are you?	Kaif halak?	Jone?
I am fine.	Ana bikhair.	Bashim.
What sports do you play?	Ay riyada tala'b?	Jewavza shek akai?
My favorite sport is soccer.	Ma riyadatak el Mofadala	Tob tobeen.

Aramaic

Aramaic was the common language of ancient Mesopotamia from about 700 B.C. to 700 A.D. Today, there are several dialects of Aramaic, each with its own script. Nestorian and Chaldean Assyrians speak an eastern dialect of Aramaic called Syriac. Other eastern dialects of Aramaic include Mandaic, which is spoken by a small population of Iraqi Mandaeans. All dialects of Aramaic are written from right to left and do not have number symbols. Instead, combinations of letters represent numbers.

Persian

The Persian language, also known as Farsi, can be traced back to the 500s B.C. It is the language of Iran, which was formerly known as Persia. It is spoken by the Persian population in Iraq, who live around Iraq's holy cities. Not only has Persian influenced the Arabic language spoken in Iraq, but more than 40 percent of modern Persian words are borrowed from Arabic. Persian is written using the Arabic script.

Turkmen

Turkmen began moving into Iraq in the 600s and now live in the north and northeast, especially near the city of Kirkuk. They speak Turkmen, a Turkic language. Most Iraqi Turkmen write their language using the Arabic script, even though a Roman-based alphabet of 28 letters was introduced for writing the language in the 1990s. No schools in Iraq currently teach in Turkmen, but the Turkmen people, as well as other Iraqi peoples, are working with the government to gain the right to be educated in both Arabic and their native languages.

This Turkmen boy serves bread at a restaurant in the northern city of Kirkuk. Kirkuk is home to Turkmen, Kurds, and Arabs. The languages of all three ethnic groups can be heard on the city's streets.

The earliest Mesopotamian writings were prayers to the gods, heroic tales, stories of battles, and **myths**. Many of these were set to music and sung at weddings, after battles, or at funerals. Storytelling was a popular pastime in Mesopotamia, and is still popular in Iraq today.

The Thousand and One Nights

The Thousand and One Nights is a collection of popular stories woven into one larger tale. The storyteller Al-Jahshiyari was most likely the first to write it down in Iraq in the 900s. *The Thousand and One Nights* tells of a woman named Scheherazade who marries the king Sharyar. Sharyar was known for marrying a new wife every day, only to have her killed the next morning. To save herself, Scheherazade told her husband a story on the very first night of their marriage, and promised to continue the next evening. The king was so enchanted by Scheherazade's stories that he allowed her to live.

Many editions of The Thousand and One Nights *have been published over the years. This illustration is from an 1895 edition.*

An ancient library

King Ashurbanipal oversaw one of the first libraries in the world, in the ancient city of Nineveh. The Assyrian king, who ruled from 668 to 627 B.C., collected Mesopotamian poems and stories, historical accounts, business contracts, government documents, and scientific texts. Archaeologists uncovered his library, complete with 25,000 clay tablets, between 1849 and 1851. These writings give a glimpse into what life was like for Sumerian, Akkadian, and Assyrian civilizations.

Modern poetry

Poetry has long been Iraq's traditional form of writing. Iraqi poems have explored love, politics, and social problems. In the 1970s, the government began to take control of the literature produced in the country. Poets and other writers were not allowed to make negative comments about the ruling Ba'th Party. Many left the country, and those who stayed were encouraged to praise their leader, Saddam Hussein, in their works. One of Iraq's best-known modern poets is Saadi Youssef, whose collections include *Without an Alphabet, Without a Face.* He left Iraq in 1979 and now lives in London, England.

Saadi Youssef's poetry has been translated into many languages. Youssef is also a respected translator of English literature into Arabic.

Bedouin poetry

The Bedouin considered their poets to be important keepers of history, honoring events and people in long, detailed stories told in verse. Poets often sang or chanted to others around the evening fire, and those listening would memorize the poems. In the 700s, a man named Hammad al-Rawiha wrote down all the Bedouin poetry he had memorized. This famous collection of verse is known as the *Mu'allaqat*.

Kurdish literature

Kurdish Iraqis are known for their fantasy stories, as well as for their chanted poems about war and love. The Kurdish poet Ahmed Khani wrote the epic *Mem-o-zin* in 1695. This love story gives a detailed look into Kurdish history and the Kurds' hopes of becoming a nation.

The Kurds, as well as Iraqi Arabs, also have a strong tradition of proverbs. The saying "What matters is the menu on the table now" stresses the importance of living in the present. "The only friends we have are the mountains" reflects the Kurdish people's history of isolation and mistreatment. Modern Kurdish literature focuses on Kurdish issues as well, such as struggles with the Iraqi government.

The Iraqi novel

Modern Iraqi novels tend to tell of life under government control, struggles between groups and individuals, and the general concerns of Arabs. Yousif al-Haydari's *Man and Cockroach*, published in 1964, tells the story of a man who is afraid of society. The novel expresses a feeling of powerlessness against the political situation of the time. Muhsin al-Ramli's book *Scattered Crumb*, published in 2003, tells of a peasant family falling apart as a father and son clash over Saddam Hussein's rule.

Iraqi author Nawal Nasrallah, who now lives in Boston, holds a copy of her cookbook Delights from the Garden of Eden: A Cookbook and a History of the Iraqi Cuisine. *Nasrallah wrote the book in the hope that it would keep Iraqi cooking alive for the many Iraqis who fled their country for the United States and other English-speaking countries.*

The Epic of Gilgamesh was discovered on 12 clay tablets in King Ashurbanipal's library at Nineveh. Written in the ancient Akkadian language, it tells of the adventures of Gilgamesh, the legendary king of the city of Uruk, who lived around 2700 B.C. After his friend Enkidu died, Gilgamesh set out to discover the secret of immortality, or everlasting life.

Gilgamesh and Utnapishtim

Gilgamesh traveled to a dark, cold land called the Far-Away to find Utnapishtim, a man who had survived a great flood in Babylon and been granted immortality. Gilgamesh hoped that Utnapishtim would share the secret of everlasting life with him.

Many rivers joined at the Far-Away before running into the ocean. By the banks of those rivers stood Utnapishtim. Gilgamesh pleaded with him, "Please, you must tell me how I can live forever, like you."

Utnapishtim sighed and looked across the rivers. "Gilgamesh, nothing is meant to live forever. Human beings are meant to live their lives, do their best, and pass on so another generation can do the same. Just like these rivers run their course and eventually end in the ocean, so too life comes to an end. Everlasting life can be lonely and terrible," he added.

Gilgamesh grew upset. "I want to live forever. You must tell me how to become immortal," he insisted.

Utnapishtim nodded his head slowly. "As you wish," he whispered. "There is a plant at the bottom of the ocean that surrounds the Far-Away. You must swim to the bottom of the ocean and snatch the plant. Eat the magic plant, and you will be young again."

Gilgamesh thanked Utnapishtim and immediately went to the water's edge. He dove into the ocean and swam with all his might to the very bottom, where he found the magic plant. Filled with joy, he rose up from the water and climbed back onto land. "I have the plant!" he announced. "Now, I shall never die."

He held the plant firmly in his hand, said goodbye to Utnapishtim, and summoned the **ferryman** to take him home. As they crossed the River of Death, Gilgamesh fell asleep. When he awoke, he wailed in despair, for in his hand he held nothing.

"Oh, gods of the heavens!" he cried. "I have lost the magic plant!"

He looked into the river just in time to see a snake disappearing into the dark water with the magic plant in his mouth. "You, serpent! You have stolen from me! Now you shall be forever young, and I shall die!"

Saddened by his loss, Gilgamesh arrived at the gates of his city, where he beheld his wonderful kingdom. The sight of all that he had built made Gilgamesh happier.

"If I cannot live forever, I must at least find a way to make a difference in the world. I will build a strong empire filled with wonderful structures. I will show the people how to be kind to one another. I will live the best way I can, so that in the end, my life will have meaning." With that, Gilgamesh approached his city with outstretched arms and peace in his heart.

Glossary

apprentice A person learning a skill by working with someone who is more experienced

archaeologist A person who studies the past by looking at buildings and artifacts

architecture The art of designing and constructing buildings

artisan A skilled craftsperson

baptize To sprinkle with water or dip in water as part of a Christian ceremony

censor To examine a book, film, or other publication in order to delete or change parts that are considered offensive

coalition A temporary political union for a particular purpose

dialect A version of a language spoken in one region

dowry The money or property that a bride brings to her groom when they marry

equinox Either of two times during the year when day and night are of equal length

ethnic Describing groups with the same nationality, customs, religion, or race

ferryman A person who transports people or goods in a boat

fertility The capacity to grow, as with plants, or have children

fortified Strengthened against attacks

glorify To make something seem more pleasant than it actually is

improvisation Something made up and performed without preparation

Latin The language of the ancient Romans

lyre An ancient string instrument resembling a harp

modesty The state of dressing and acting in a proper, respectable way

monarchy A government that is ruled by a king, queen, emperor, or empress

mosaic A design made from small pieces of stone, glass, or tile

mystical Spiritual

myth A traditional story about a god or another being with superhuman powers

nomadic Having no fixed home and moving from place to place in search of food and water

Ottoman A member of a Turkish dynasty

pagan Related to a belief in spirits in nature

pilgrimage A religious journey to a sacred place

prophet A person believed to deliver messages from God

reflection Careful thought

republic A country led by an elected government rather than a king or queen

ritual A religious ceremony in which steps must be followed in a certain order

rival Opposing

sacrifice The act of killing an animal in a religious ceremony as an offering to the gods

scribe A person who copies manuscripts and documents

shrine A holy place dedicated to a god or saint

temple A building used for religious services

underworld The imaginary place of the dead below the earth

Zoroastrian Related to a religion that was developed in ancient Iran by the prophet Zoroaster. It is based on the idea that there is a continuous fight between a god who represents good and one who represents evil

 # Index